GRANDMA MARGIE'S TALE OF LOVING NEIGHBOR: THE STORY OF THE GOOD SAMARITAN

Written By Dr. K.T. Zulkowski

Published by Mz. Kim Productions

4263 Tierra Rejada Rd #151

Moorpark, CA 93021

www.mzkimproductions.com

ISBN: 978-1-962106-21-4

Printed in United States of America

First Printing: November 2023

Date of Copyright: July 5,2023

For permissions, please contact: Mz. Kim Productions

4263 Tierra Rejada Rd #151

Moorpark, CA 93021

www.mzkimproductions.com

mzkimproductions@gmail.com

Dedication

This book is dedicated to all the unsung heroes who, with their small acts of kindness, make this world a better place. To the teachers who inspire, the parents who nurture, and the friends who support – your love and kindness are the foundation of our communities.

And a special dedication to my dear Grandma Margie, whose stories of love, compassion, and neighborliness have not only shaped this book but also my life. Your wisdom continues to guide us, reminding us of the power of love in its simplest form.

May the tales in this book inspire every reader to spread love, kindness, and empathy, just as you have done.

With all my love,

Dr. K.T. Zulkowski

Educational Value

"Grandma Margie's Tale of Loving Neighbor" offers significant educational value across multiple domains:

1. **Character Education**: The story instills important values such as kindness, empathy, and love. It teaches children to respect and care for everyone, regardless of their differences, fostering a broad sense of inclusivity and understanding.

2. **Social-Emotional Learning**: The narrative promotes empathy and compassion, teaching children to recognize and respond to the needs of those around them. This helps them develop emotional intelligence, nurturing their ability to understand and manage emotions.

3. **Critical Thinking**: By prompting readers to consider how they can be a good neighbor in their own lives, it encourages critical thinking and self-reflection. This aids in the development of problem-solving skills and decision-making abilities.

4. **Civic Responsibility**: The story inspires children to participate in community service and small acts of kindness. This nurtures a sense of responsibility towards their community, teaching them the importance of contributing towards societal well-being.

. **Religious Education**: The inclusion of Bible verses and the parable of the Good Samaritan provide a spiritual foundation for the story, offering opportunities for meaningful discussions about faith and the teachings of Jesus.

. **Literacy Skills**: Besides its thematic educational value, the book also contributes to the development of literacy skills. Through engaging narrative and dialogue, children can improve their reading comprehension, vocabulary, and language skills.

n essence, "Grandma Margie's Tale of Loving Neighbor" serves as a comprehensive educational tool, aiding in character development, social-emotional learning, and fostering a sense of civic duty, all while strengthening literacy skills.

Once upon a time, in a peaceful village filled with love and kindness, lived two curious and compassionate grandchildren named Zion and Zipporah. They loved spending time with their wise and loving Grandma Margie. One sunny afternoon, as they sat beside her on a cozy bench, Grandma Margie had a special story to share.

"Children," Grandma Margie said with a warm smile, "I want to tell you a story that Jesus once shared with His followers. It's a story about being a loving neighbor and showing kindness to others."

"Long ago," Grandma Margie began, "there was a man who was traveling from Jerusalem to Jericho. Along the way, he was attacked by robbers who left him hurt and helpless."

Zion asked, "What happened next, Grandma?"

Grandma Margie continued, "Several people passed by, but they didn't stop to help. They were too busy or afraid. But then, a Samaritan man came along."

"Samaritans and Jews didn't usually get along," Grandma Margie explained. "But this Samaritan showed great love and compassion. He bandaged the man's wounds, lifted him onto his donkey, and took him to an inn."

Zipporah asked, "Why did the Samaritan help him, Grandma?"

"Because he understood the importance of loving our neighbors," Grandma Margie replied. "He saw someone in need and chose to show kindness, regardless of their differences."

Grandma Margie continued, "The next day, the Samaritan had to continue his journey, but before he left, he made sure the innkeeper would take care of the injured man. He even promised to return and pay for any additional expenses."

Zion exclaimed, "That's amazing, Grandma! The Samaritan truly loved his neighbor!"

"And just like the Good Samaritan, we can be loving neighbors too," Grandma Margie continued. "We can show kindness, help those in need, and treat everyone with love and respect."

Bible Verses:

- "Love your neighbor as yourself." (Mark 12:31)

- "But a Samaritan, as he traveled, came where the man was; and when he saw him, he took pity on him." (Luke 10:33)

- "Go and do likewise." (Luke 10:37)

Grandma Margie said, "Let's remember the words of Jesus and His teachings about loving our neighbors. The Bible tells us to love others as we love ourselves."

Zion asked, "How can we be loving neighbors, Grandma?"

Grandma Margie replied, "We can start by being kind, helping those in need, and treating everyone with respect. Small acts of love can make a big difference."

Zipporah suggested, "We can visit the elderly in our community and spend time with them. They would appreciate our company and care."

Grandma Margie added, "We can also volunteer at local shelters or donate food and clothes to those who are less fortunate. Every little act of kindness counts."

Zion said, "I want to be a loving neighbor, just like the Samaritan. I want to help people and make them feel loved."

Grandma Margie hugged Zion and said, "That's a beautiful heart, my dear. Your kindness will touch many lives."

Zipporah suggested, "We can also take care of our environment by planting trees and flowers. It shows love for our planet and the creatures that live here."

Grandma Margie smiled and said, "Caring for our planet is indeed an act of love. It's important to be good stewards of the Earth."

Zion exclaimed, "I can't wait to start being a loving neighbor and making a positive impact in our community

Grandma Margie replied, "I'm proud of you, my dear. Your love and kindness will inspire others to do the same

Grandma Margie concluded, "Remember, my dear grandchildren, being a loving neighbor is a lifelong journey. Let's continue to spread love, kindness, and compassion wherever we go."

Grandma Margie concluded, "Remember, my dear grandchildren, being a loving neighbor is a lifelong journey. Let's continue to spread love, kindness, and compassion wherever we go."

Author's Note

Author's Note:

Writing "Grandma Margie's Tale of Loving Neighbor" has been an enriching and fulfilling journey for me. As an author and an educator, I have always believed in the power of stories to inspire and educate our young minds. This book is a labor of love, born from the desire to share the timeless story of the Good Samaritan in a way that appeals to the young, curious minds of today.

I have always admired the teachings of Jesus, particularly the parable of the Good Samaritan, which offers a profound message of love, kindness, and empathy. I wanted to create a story that not only entertains children but also holds significant educational value. My hope is that through Grandma Margie, Zion, and Zipporah, children will understand the importance of being a loving neighbor and showing kindness to others, regardless of their differences.

The inclusion of Bible verses is meant to reinforce the teachings of Jesus and provide a spiritual foundation for the story. These verses can spark meaningful discussions about faith, love, and the significance of treating others with respect and care.

In writing this book, my ultimate objective was to encourage critical thinking and reflection among young readers. The story prompts them to consider how they can be loving neighbors in their own lives and communities. It is my earnest hope that the book will inspire children to take action, whether it's through small acts of kindness or participating in community service projects.

"Grandma Margie's Tale of Loving Neighbor" is more than just a story; it's a tool aimed at fostering character development and social-emotional learning. It is my sincere hope that this book will empower children to make a positive impact in the world around them, instilling in them the important values of love, kindness, and empathy.

Thank you for joining me on this journey. I hope you and your young ones enjoy reading "Grandma Margie's Tale of Loving Neighbor" as much as I enjoyed writing it.

Warmly,

Dr. K.T. Zulkowski